C.H.G.   .M.J.

This boo[...]ly the scientif[...]oman Catholic Fa[...]better serve God, drawing particularly on that gigantic source of God's Infinite Goodness and Mercy - a source virtually untapped: Prophetic Revelations.

"When it's a question of prophetic revelations the Pope is the sole judge!" Pope Leo X (5th Council of Lateran 1513)

DEDICATION

The Blessed Virgin said: "You love Me and make others love Me." This revised edition of the Pieta Prayer Booklet is dedicated to you Dear Lady of Ephesus as an act of love to honour your Assumption. "I am all yours, my Queen and Mother and all that I have is yours".

PURPOSE

Scripture says: "Pray without ceasing." St. Paul of the Cross wrote: "We enter on the broad road of perdition when we neglect prayer." Dr. Alexis Carrel wrote: "If you make a habit of prayer, your life will be profoundly altered." As a scientist he turned to prayer as man's highest activity; that conversation with God to be an art of all arts.

May this Pieta Prayer Booklet serve as a spiritual tool for souls who wish to increase their daily prayer life. May the Dear Angels who carried the Holy House of Loreto carry this booklet to all persons who wish to pray more after reciting the daily rosary.

Most Sacred Heart of Jesus, have mercy on us.

Immaculate Heart of Mary, pray for us.

Imprimatur
Francis Cardinal Spellman
Archbishop New York

NIHIL Obstat
John M.A. Fearns, S.T.D., P.A.
Censor Librorum

The Fifteen Prayers revealed by Our Lord to Saint Bridget of Sweden in the Church of St. Paul of Rome

PRAYERS

approved by Pope Pius IX
Magnificent Promises to Saint Bridget of Sweden

Pope Benedict XV expressed himself as followed on the Revelations of St. Bridget: "The approbation of such revelations implies nothing more than, after mature examination, it is permissible to publish them for the same credence as the truths of religion, one can, however, believe them out of human faith, conforming to the rules of prudence by which they are probable, and supported by sufficient motives that one might believe in them piously. (Les Petitis Bollandistes, tome XII)

The 14th of June 1303, at the moment Bridget was born, Benedict, the curate of Rasbo, prayed for the happy deliverance of Ingeborde. Suddenly he found himself enveloped by a luminous cloud out of which Our Lady appeared.

"A child has been born at Birger; her voice will be heard by the entire world."

Sagii, die XXIV Aprilis 1903
Imprimatur F.J. Girard, V.G.

These prayers and these promises have been copied from a book printed in Toulouse in 1740 and published by the P. Adrien Parvilliers of the Company of Jesus, Apostolic Missionary of the Holy Land, with approbation, permission and recommendation to distribute them.

Parents and teachers who will read them to young infants for at least one year will assure their being preserved for life from any grave accident which would involve the loss of one of their five senses.

Pope Pius IX took cognisance of these prayers with the prologue; he approved them May 31, 1862, recognising them as true and for the good of souls.

This sentence of Pope Pius IX has been confirmed by the realisation of the promises by all persons who have recited the prayers and by numerous supernatural facts by which God wanted to make known their exact truth. A collection of small books, these prayers among them, were approved by the Great congress of Malines on August 22, 1863.

Question - Must one recite the prayers everyday without interruption to obtain the privileges?

Answer - One should miss saying them as few times as possible; but if for a serious reason one is obliged to miss them, one doesn't lose the privileges attached to them, as long as one recites 5480 prayers during the year. One must say them with devotion and concentrate on the words one pronounces. These prayers can serve as the Way of the Cross.

Visitors to the Church of St. Paul at Rome can see the Crucifix, above the Tabernacle in the Blessed Sacrament Chapel, sculptured by Pierre Cavallini, before which St. Bridget knelt when she received these 15 Prayers from our Lord. The following inscription is placed in the church to commemorate the event: "Pendentis, Pendente Dei verba accepit aure accipit et verbum corde Brigitta Deum. Anno Jubilei MCCCL."

As St. Bridget for a long time wanted to know the number of blows Our Lord received during His Passion, He one day appeared to her and said: "I received 5480 blows on My Body. If you wish to honour them in some way, say 15 Our Fathers and 15 Hail Marys with the following prayers (which He taught her) for a whole year. When the year is up, you will have honoured each one of My Wounds".

Our Lord made the following promises to anyone who recited the 15 St. Bridget Prayers for a whole year.

Promises

1. I will deliver 15 souls of their lineage from Purgatory.

2. 15 souls of their lineage will be confirmed and preserved in grace.

3. 15 sinners of their lineage will be converted.

4. Whoever recites these prayers will attain the first degree of perfection.

5. 15 days before their death I will give them My Precious Body in order that they may escape eternal starvation; I will give them My Precious Blood to drink lest they thirst eternally.

6. 15 days before their death they will feel a deep contrition for all their sins and will have a perfect knowledge of them.

7. I will place before them the sign of My Victorious Cross for their help and defence against the attacks of their enemies.

8. Before their death I shall come with My Dearest Beloved Mother.

9. I shall graciously receive their soul, and will lead it into eternal joy.

10. And having led it there I shall give them a special draught from the fountain of My Deity, something I will not do for those who have not recited My Prayers.

11. Let it be known that whoever may have been living in a state of mortal sin for 30 years, but who will recite devoutly, or have the intention to recite these Prayers, the Lord will forgive them all their sins.

12. I shall protect them from strong temptations.

13. I shall preserve and guard their 5 senses.

14. I shall preserve them from a sudden death.

15. Their soul will be delivered from eternal death.

16. They will obtain all they ask for from God and the Blessed Virgin.

17. If they have lived all their life doing their own will and they are to die the next day, their life will be prolonged.

18. Every time one recites these Prayers they gain 100 days indulgence.

19. They are assured of being joined to the supreme Choir of Angels.

20. Whoever teaches these Prayers to another, will have continuous joy and merit which will endure eternally.

21. Where these Prayers are being said or will be said in the future God is present with His grace.

First Prayer

Our Father - Hail Mary. O Jesus Christ! Eternal Sweetness to those who love You, joy surpassing all joy and all desire, Salvation and Hope of all sinners, You have proved that You have no greater desire than to be among men, even assuming human nature at the fullness of time for the love of men, recall all the sufferings You have endured from the instant of Your conception, and especially during Your Passion, as it was decreed and ordained from all eternity in the Divine plan.

Remember, O Lord, that during the Last Supper with Your disciples, having washed their feet, You gave them Your Most Precious Body and Blood, and while at the same time You did sweetly console them, You did foretell of Your coming Passion.

Remember, the sadness and bitterness which You did experience in Your Soul as You Yourself bore witness saying: "My Soul is sorrowful even unto death".

Remember all the fear, anguish and pain that You did suffer in Your delicate Body before the torment of the Crucifixion, when, after having prayed three times, bathed in a sweat of blood, You were betrayed by Judas, Your disciple, arrested by the people of a nation You had chosen and elevated, accused by false witnesses, unjustly judged by their judges during the flower of Your youth and during the solemn Paschal season.

Remember that You were despoiled of Your garments and clothed in those of derision; that Your Face and Eyes were veiled, that You were buffeted, crowned with thorns, a reed placed in Your Hands, that You were crushed with blows and overwhelmed with affronts and outrages.

In memory of all these pains and sufferings which You did endure before Your Passion on the Cross, grant me before my death true contrition, a sincere and entire confession, worthy satisfaction and the remission of all my sins. Amen.

Second Prayer

Our Father - Hail Mary. O Jesus! True liberty of angels, Paradise of delights, remember the horror and sadness which You did endure when Your enemies, like furious lions, surrounded You, and by thousands of insults, spits, blows, lacerations and other unheard-of cruelties, tormented You at will. In consideration of these torments and insulting words, I beseech You, O my Saviour, to deliver me from all my enemies, visible and invisible and to bring me, under Your protection, to the perfection of eternal salvation, Amen.

Third Prayer

Our Father - Hail Mary. O Jesus! Creator of Heaven and earth Whom nothing can encompass or limit, You Who do enfold and hold all under Your Loving power, remember the very bitter pain You did suffer when the Jews nailed Your Sacred Hands and Feet to the Cross blow after blow with big blunt nails, and not finding You in a pitiable enough state to satisfy their rage, they enlarged Your Wounds, and added pain to pain, and with indescribable cruelty stretched Your Body on the Cross, pulled You from all sides, thus dislocating Your Limbs. I beg of You, O Jesus, by the memory of this most loving suffering of the Cross, to grant me the grace to fear You and to Love You. Amen.

Fourth Prayer

Our Father - Hail Mary. O Jesus! Heavenly Physician, raised aloft on the Cross to heal our wounds with Yours, remember the bruises which You did suffer and the weakness of all Your members which were distended to such a degree that never was there pain like Yours. From the crown on Your Head to the Soles of Your Feet there was not one spot on Your Body that was not in torment, and yet, forgetting all Your sufferings, You did not cease to pray to Your Heavenly Father for Your enemies saying: "Father forgive them for they know not what they do".

Through this great Mercy, and in memory of this suffering, grant that the remembrance of Your Most Bitter Passion may effect in us a perfect contrition and the remission of all our sins. Amen.

Fifth Prayer

Our Father - Hail Mary. O Jesus! Mirror of eternal splendour, remember the sadness which You experienced, when contemplating in the light of Your Divinity and predestination of those who would be saved by the merits of Your Sacred Passion, You did see at the same time, the great multitude of reprobates who would be damned for their sins, and You did complain bitterly of those hopeless lost and unfortunate sinners. Through this abyss of compassion and pity, and especially through the goodness which You displayed to the good thief when You said to him: "This day, You shall be with Me in Paradise." I beg of You, O Sweet Jesus, that at the hour of my death, You will show me mercy too. Amen.

Sixth Prayer

Our Father - Hail Mary. O Jesus! Beloved and most desirable King, remember the grief You did suffer, when naked and like a common criminal, You were fastened and raised on the Cross, when all Your relatives and friends abandoned You, except Your Beloved Mother, who remained close to You during Your agony and whom You did entrust to

Your faithful disciple when You said to Mary: "Woman, behold your son!" and to St. John: "Son, behold Your Mother!"

Ibeg of You O my Saviour, by the sword of sorrow which pierced the soul of Your holy Mother, to have compassion on me in all my afflictions and tribulations, both corporal and spiritual, and to assist me in all my trials, and especially at the hour of my death. Amen.

Seventh Prayer

Our Father - Hail Mary. O Jesus! Inexhaustible Fountain of compassion, Who by a profound gesture of Love, said from the Cross: "I thirst!" suffered with a thirst for the salvation of the human race. I beg of You O my Saviour, to inflame in our hearts the desire to tend towards perfection in all our acts and to extinguish in us the excessive desire of the flesh and the love of worldly things. Amen.

Eighth Prayer

Our Father - Hail Mary. O Jesus! Sweetness of Hearts, delight of the spirit, by the bitterness of the vinegar and gall which You did taste on the Cross for Love of us, grant us the grace to receive worthily Your Precious Body and Blood during our life and at the hour of our death, that they may serve as a remedy and consolation for our souls. Amen.

Ninth Prayer

Our Father - Hail Mary. O Jesus! Royal virtue, joy of the mind, recall the pain You did endure when, plunged in an ocean of bitterness at the approach of death, insulted and outraged, You did cry out in a loud voice that You were abandoned by Your Father, saying "My God, My God, why hast thou forsaken me ? Through this anguish, I beg of You, O my Saviour, not to abandon me in the terrors and pains of my death. Amen.

Tenth Prayer

Our Father - Hail Mary. O Jesus! Who art the beginning and end of all things, life and virtue, remember that for our sakes You were plunged in an abyss of suffering from the soles of Your Feet to the crown of Your Head. In consideration of the enormity of Your Wounds, teach me to keep, through pure love, Your Commandments, whose ways are wide and easy for those who love you. Amen.

Eleventh Prayer

Our Father - Hail Mary. O Jesus! Deep abyss of mercy, I beg of You, in memory of Your Wounds which penetrated to the very marrow of Your Bones and to the depth of Your Being, to draw me, a miserable sinner, overwhelmed by my offenses, away from sin and to hide me from Your Face justly irritated against me, hide me in

Your Wounds, until Your anger and just indignation shall have passed away. Amen.

Twelfth Prayer

Our Father - Hail Mary. O Jesus! Mirror of Truth, Symbol of Unity, Link of Charity, remember the multitude of wounds with which You were covered from head to foot, torn and reddened by the spilling of Your adorable Blood. O Great and Universal Pain which You did suffer in Your virginal Flesh for Love of us! Sweetest Jesus! What is there that You could have done for us which You have not done! May the fruit of Your sufferings be renewed in my soul by the faithful remembrance of Your Passion and may Your Love increase in my heart each day, until I see You in eternity.

You who are the treasury of every real good and every joy, which I beg You to grant me, O Sweetest Jesus, in Heaven, Amen.

Thirteenth Prayer

Our Father - Hail Mary. O Jesus! Strong Lion, Immortal and Invincible King, remember the pain which You did endure when all Your strength, both moral and physical, was entirely exhausted, You did bow Your Head, saying: "It is consummated" Through this anguish and grief, I beg of You Lord Jesus, to have mercy on me at the hour of my death when my mind will be greatly troubled and my soul will be in anguish. Amen.

Fourteenth Prayer

Our Father - Hail Mary. O Jesus! Only Son of the Father, Splendour and Figure of His Substance, remember the simple and humble recommendation You did make of Your Soul to Your Eternal Father, saying: "Father, into Your Hands I commend my Spirit!" And with Your Body all torn, and Your Heart Broken, and the bowels of Your Mercy open to redeem us, You did Expire. By this Precious Death, I beg of You O King of Saints, comfort me and help me to resist the devil, the flesh and the world, so that being dead to the world I may live for You alone. I beg of You at the hour of my death to receive me, a pilgrim and an exile returning to You. Amen.

Fifteenth Prayer

Our Father - Hail Mary. O Jesus! True and fruitful Vine! Remember the abundant outpouring of Blood which You did so generously shed from Your Sacred Body as juice from grapes in a wine press. From Your Side, pierced with a lance by a soldier, blood and water issued forth until there was not left in Your Body a single drop, and finally, like a bundle of myrrh lifted to the top of the Cross Your delicate Flesh was destroyed, the very Substance of Your body withered, and the Marrow of Your Bones dried up. Through this bitter Passion and through the outpouring of Your Precious Blood, I beg of You, O Sweet Jesus, to receive my soul when I am in my death agony. Amen.

Conclusion

OSweet Jesus! Pierce my heart so that my tears of penitence and love will be my bread day and night; may I be converted entirely to You, may my heart be Your perpetual habitation, may my conversation be pleasing to You, and may the end of my life be so praiseworthy that I may merit Heaven and there with Your saints, praise You forever, Amen.

Promises to those who sing

"Ave Maris Stella"

During a riot at Rome, a mob came to the house where St. Bridget lived: a leader talked of burning Bridget alive. She prayed to Our Lord to know if she should flee to safety. Jesus advised her stay: "It doesn't matter if they plot Your death. My power will break the malice of Your enemies: if Mine crucified Me, it is because I permitted it". Our Blessed Mother added: "Sing as a group the AVE MARIS STELLA and I'll guard you from every danger".

Ave Maris Stella	Hail thou Star of Ocean
Dei Mater alma,	Portal of the Sky
Atque semper virgo,	Ever Virgin Mother
Felix coeli porta	Of the Lord Most High

Sumens illud ave	O! by Gabriel's Ave,
Gabrielis ore,	Uttered long ago,
Funda nos in pace,	Eva's name reversing
Mutans Evae nomen	Established peace below.
Solve vincla reis	Break the captives' fetters,
Profer lumen caecis	Light on blindness pour,
Mala nostra pelle,	All our ills expelling,
Bona cuncta posce.	Every bliss implore
Monstra te esse Matrem	Show thyself a Mother,
Sumat per te preces	Offer Him our sighs,
Qui pro nobis natus	Who for us incarnate
Tulit esse tuus	Did not thee despise
Virgo singularis	Virgin of all Virgins
Inter omnes mitis	To thy shelter take us,
Nos culpis solutos	Gentlest of the gentle
Mites fac et castos.	Chaste and gentle make us.
Vitam presta puram	Still, as on we journey
Iter para tutum,	Help our weak endeavour,
Ut, videntes Jesum	Till with thee and Jesus
Semper Collaetemur	We rejoice forever
Sit laus Deo Patri,	Through the highest heaven,
Summo Cristo decus	To the almighty Three
Spiritui sancto:	Father, Son, and Spirit,
Tribus honor unus.	One same glory be.
Amen	Amen.

TO THE BLESSED VIRGIN

My Queen, my Mother, I give myself entirely to you and to show my devotion to you, I consecrate to you this day, my eyes, my ears, my mouth, my heart, my whole being without reserve. Wherefore good Mother as I am Yours keep me, guard me, as your property and possession. Amen.

"An indulgence of 500 days"

My daily Offering

O Jesus, through the Immaculate Heart of Mary, I offer You my prayers, works, joys sufferings of this day in union with the Holy Sacrifice of the Mass throughout the world. I offer them for all the intentions of Your Sacred Heart: the salvation of souls, reparation for sin, the union of all Christians. I offer them for the intentions of our Bishops and of all Apostles of Prayer,and in particular for those recommended by our Holy Father this month.

*Angel of God My guardian dear
To whom His love commits me here
Ever this day be at my side
To light and guard
To rule and guide. Amen*

"Say daily upon arising, 7 Glory Be's to your guardian angel"

Prayer to St. Joseph over 1900 years old

O St. Joseph whose protection is so great, so strong, so prompt before the Throne of God, I place in you all my interests and desires. O St. Joseph do assist me by your powerful intercession and obtain for me from your Divine Son all spiritual blessings through Jesus Christ, Our Lord; so that having engaged here below your Heavenly power I may offer my Thanksgiving and Homage to the most Loving of Fathers. O St. Joseph, I never weary contemplating you with Jesus asleep in your arms. I dare not approach while He reposes near your heart. Press Him in my name and kiss His fine Head for me, and ask Him to return the Kiss when I draw my dying breath. St. Joseph, Patron of departing souls, pray for us. Amen.

Say for nine consecutive mornings for anything you may desire. It has seldom been known to fail.

This prayer was found in the fiftieth year of Our Lord Jesus Christ. In the 1500's it was sent by the Pope to the Emperor Charles when he was going into battle.

Whoever reads this prayer or hears it or carries it, will never die a sudden death, nor be drowned, nor will poison take effect on them. They will not fall into the hands of the enemy nor be burned in any fire, nor will they be defeated in battle.

Make this prayer known everywhere.

Imprimatur.
Most Rev. George V. Ahr
Bishop of Trenton

Glory Be To Jesus and Mary

A letter written by the Blessed Virgin Mary to the City of Messina where St. Paul, the Apostle preached the gospel, which has been preserved in the Reliquary of the great altar.

"I, Mary, Virgin, servant of God, very humble Mother of Jesus Christ, Son of God, the Almighty and Eternity, to all who are in Messina, health and benediction in our Lord. You have learned by the ambassadors who have been sent to you. You received the gospel and you acknowledged that the son of God has become man, and has suffered the passion and death for the salvation of the world, and that He is Christ and also the true Messiah. I beseech you to persevere, promising to you and all your posterity, to assist you in the presence of My Son."

Mary Virgin, very humble servant of God
(Great graces are given to those who carry a copy of this letter.)

Prayer for Daily Neglects

Eternal Father, I offer You the Sacred Heart of Jesus, with all its Love, all its Sufferings and all its Merits.

First -   To expiate all the sins I have committed this day and during all my life. Glory be to the Father and to the Son...!

Second -   To purify the good I have done badly this day and during all my life. Glory be to the Father and to the Son...!

Third -   To supply for the good I ought to have done, and that I have neglected this day and during all my life. Glory be to the Father and to the Son..!

A Poor Clare nun, who had just died, appeared to her abbess, who was praying for her, and said to her, "I went straight to heaven, for, by means of this prayer, recited every evening, I paid my debts."

(This prayer is not meant to replace confession)

Hail Mary of Gold

Hail Mary, White Lily of the Glorious and always serene Trinity. Hail brilliant Rose of the Garden of heavenly delights.

O you, by whom God wanted to be born and by whose milk the King of Heaven wanted to be nourished! Nourish our souls with effusions of divine grace. Amen!

At the hour when the soul which has thus greeted me quits the body I'll appear to them in such splendid beauty that they'll taste, to their great consolation, something of the joys of Paradise.

The Blessed Virgin Mary to St. Gertrude the Great (Revelations book III, chapter XVIII).

Saint Gertrude's Prayer for Souls in Purgatory

(a prayer which would release souls from Purgatory each time it is said)

Eternal Father, I offer Thee the Most Precious Blood of Thy Divine Son, Jesus, in union with all the Masses said throughout the world today, for all the souls in Purgatory, for sinners everywhere, for sinners in the Universal Church, those in my own home and within my family. Amen

This picture of Our Lady was drawn by a
mystic in Italy. Her hand was guided by
Our Lady.

There is a special blessing given each day to
the person who carries it and another blessing
given each time one looks at it with love.

Which are very useful to a dying person, and should be prayed often as an act of mercy.

There once was a Pope in Rome who was surrounded by many sins. The Lord God struck him with a fatal illness. When he saw that he was dying he summoned Cardinals, Bishops and learned persons and said to them: "My dear friends! What comfort can you give me now that I must die, and when I deserve eternal damnation for my sins"? No one answered him. One of them, a pious curate named John, said:

"Father, why do you doubt the Mercy of God?" The Pope replied: "What comfort can you give me now that I must die and fear that I'll be damned for my sins?"

John replied: "I'll read three prayers over you; I hope you'll be comforted and that you'll obtain Mercy from God."

The Pope was unable to say more. The curate and all those present knelt and said an Our Father, then the following Prayers:

1. Prayer

Lord Jesus Christ! Thou Son of God and Son of the Virgin Mary, God and Man, You who in fear sweated blood for us on the Mount of Olives in order to bring peace, and to offer thy most Holy death to God Thy Heavenly Father for the salvation of this dying person...If it be, however, that by his sins he merits eternal damnation, then may it be deflected from him. This, oh Eternal Father, through Our Lord Jesus Christ, Thy Dear Son, Who liveth and reigneth in union with The Holy Spirit now and forever. Amen.

2. Prayer

Lord Jesus Christ! You Who meekly died on the trunk of the Cross for us, submitting Thy Will completely to Thy Heavenly Father in order to bring peace and to offer Thy most Holy death to Thy Heavenly Father in order to free...(this person) and to hide from him what he has earned with his sins; grant this, oh Eternal Father, through Our Lord Jesus Thy Son, Who liveth and reigneth with Thee in union with the Holy Spirit now and forever. Amen.

3. Prayer

Lord Jesus Christ! Thou Who remained silent to speak through the mouths of the Prophets: I have drawn Thee to me through Eternal Love, which Love drew Thee from Heaven into the body of The Virgin, which love drew Thee from the body of The Virgin into the valley of this needful world, which Love kept Thee 33 years in this world, and as a sign of Great Love, Thou hast given Thy Holy Body as True Food and Thy Holy Blood as True drink as a sign of Great Love, Thou has consented to be a prisoner and to be led from one judge to another and as a sign of Great Love Thou hast consented to be condemned to death, and hast consented to die and to be buried and truly risen, and appeared to Thy Holy Mother and all the Holy Apostles, and as a sign of Great Love Thou has ascended, under Thy own Strength and Power, and sitteth at the Right Hand of God Thy Heavenly Father, and Thou has sent Thy Holy Spirit into the hearts of Thy Apostles and the hearts of all who hope and believe in Thee. Through Thy Sign of Eternal Love, open Heaven today and take this dying person whose sins have been forgiven into the Realm of Thy Heavenly Father, that he may reign with Thee now and forever. Amen.

Meanwhile the Pope died. The curate persevered to the third hour, then the Pope appeared to him in body and comforting him; his countenance as brilliant as the sun, his clothes as white as snow, and he said: "My dear brother! Whereas I was supposed to be a child of damnation I've become a child of happiness. As you recited the first Prayer many of my sins fell from me as rain from Heaven, and as you recited the second Prayer I was purified, as a goldsmith purifies gold in a hot fire. I was still further purified as you recited the third Prayer. Then I saw Heaven open and the Lord Jesus standing on the Right Hand of God the Father Who said to me: "Come, all thy sins are forgiven thee, you will remain in the Realm of My Father forever. Amen."

With these words my soul separated from my body and the Angels of God led it to Eternal Joy.

As the curate heard this he said: "O Holy Father! I can't tell these things to anyone, for they won't believe me". Then the Pope said: "Truly I tell thee, the Angel of God stands with me and has written the prayers in letters of gold for the consolement of all sinners. If a person had committed all the sins in the world, but that the three Prayers shall have been read (over him) at his end (death), all his sins will be forgiven him, even though his soul was supposed to suffer until the Last Judgment, it will be redeemed (freed).

The person who hears them read, he won't die an unhappy death, also in whose house they will be read. Therefore take these prayers and carry them into St. Peter's Basilica and lay them in the Chapel named the Assumption of Mary, for certain consolation. The person who will be near death, who reads them or hears them read gains 400 years indulgence for the days he was supposed to suffer in Purgatory because of his guilt. Also who reads this Prayer or hears it read, the hour of his death shall be revealed to him. Amen!

AN ACT OF CONTRITION

O my God, I am heartily sorry for all my sins, because of them I deserve the eternal pains of Hell, but most of all because I have offended Thee my God who art all - good and deserving of all my love. I firmly resolve with the help of Thy grace to confess my sins, to do penance, to avoid the proximate occasion of sin and never to sin anymore. Amen.

Tips on Prayer

Your prayers are strongest at the consecration in Holy Mass (raising of Host and Chalice). Each time we look at The Most Blessed Sacrament our place in Heaven is raised forever. (revealed by Our Lord to St. Gertrude the Great.)

Prayer to Obtain the Grace of All World's Masses

Eternal Father, we humbly offer Thee our poor presence and that of the whole of humanity from the beginning to the end of the world at all the Masses that ever have or ever will be prayed. We offer Thee all the pains, suffering, prayers, sacrifices, joys and relaxations of our lives, in union with those of our dear Lord Jesus here on earth. May the Most Precious Blood of Christ, all His Blood and wounds and agony save us, through the sorrowful and Immaculate Heart of Mary. Amen! (This prayer should be prayed daily, and made known.)

Dear St. Philomena pray for us for that purity of mind and heart which lead to the Perfect Love of God!

God must be pursued and the more you chase Him the more you catch Him (Maimonedes).

Graces Derived from Assisting at Mass

1. The Mass is Calvary continued.
2. Every Mass is worth as much as the sacrifice of Our Lord's life, suffering and death.
3. Holy Mass is the most powerful atonement for your sins.
4. At the hour of death the Masses you have heard will be your greatest consolation.
5. Every Mass will go with you to judgment and plead for pardon.
6. At Mass you can diminish more or less temporal punishment due to your sins, according to your fervour.
7. Assisting devoutly at Holy Mass you render to the sacred humanity of Our Lord the greatest homage.
8. He supplies for many of your negligences and omissions.
9. He forgives the venial sins which you have not confessed. The power of Satan over you is diminished.

10. You afford the souls in Purgatory the greatest possible relief.
11. One Mass heard during life will be of more benefit to you than many heard for you after your death.
12. You are preserved from dangers and misfortunes which otherwise might have befallen you. You shorten your Purgatory.
13. Every Mass wins for you a higher degree of glory in Heaven.
14. You receive the priest's blessing which Our Lord ratifies in Heaven.
15. You kneel amidst a multitude of holy angels, who are present at the adorable Sacrifice with reverential awe.
16. You are blessed in your temporal goods and affairs.

In eternity, we shall fully realise that it was certainly worthwhile to have assisted at Holy Mass daily.

PRAY FOR PRIESTS THAT THEY MAY OFFER THE MASS WITH HOLY LOVE AND REVERENCE.

St. Bonaventure said: "that whoever neglected Our Lady would perish in his sins and would be damned."

HOLY COMMUNION

Each time we receive Holy Communion our venial sins are forgiven.

Christ revealed to St. Gertrude the Great that each time one person receives Holy Communion something good happens to every being in heaven on earth and in purgatory.

The Cure of Ars said that a Communion well received is worth more than 20,000 Francs given to the poor.

Each time we receive Communion our place in heaven is raised forever, our stay in purgatory shortened.

WE SHOULD NEVER LET A DAY PASS WITHOUT GOING TO HOLY COMMUNION!

Spiritual Communion

The value of a spiritual Communion well made is enormous. We can and should make one frequently. Simply think on Jesus and how much He loves us and how much we love Him, then ask Our Blessed Mother to ask Her Divine Son to come into our hearts. We can offer these Communions for the interest of the Sorrowful and Immaculate Heart of Mary, noting our special intention!

After receiving Holy Communion Our Lord said we should pray: "Most Sacred Heart of Jesus may the whole world burn with love for You! (revelation to Gabrielle Bossis in France).

A True Letter of Our Saviour Jesus Christ

Consecrating the Drops of Blood which Our Lord Jesus lost on His way to Calvary.

Copy of a letter of the Oration found in the Holy Sepulchre of Our Lord Jesus Christ in Jerusalem, preserved in a silver box by His Holiness and by the Emperors and Empresses of the Christian Faith.

St. Elizabeth, Queen of Hungary, with St. Matilda and St. Bridget, wishing to know something of the Passion of Jesus Christ, offered fervent and special prayers, upon which there appeared to them Our Lord Jesus Christ who spoke to them in the following manner:

I descended from Heaven to the Earth in order to convert you.

In olden times people were religious and their harvests were abundant; at present, on the contrary, they are scanty.

If you want to reap an abundant harvest you must not work on Sunday, for on Sunday you must go to church and pray to God to forgive your sins. He gave you six days in which to work and one for rest and devotion and to render your help to the poor and assist the Church.

Those people, who brawl against my religion and cast slurs on this Sacred Letter, shall be forsaken by me.

On the contrary, those people who shall carry a copy of this letter with them shall be free from death by drowning and from sudden death. They shall be free from all contagious diseases and lightning; they shall not die without confession, and shall be free from their enemies and from the hand of wrongful authority, and from all their slanderers and false witnesses.

Women in peril at childbirth will, by keeping this Oration about them, immediately overcome the difficulty. In the houses where this Oration is kept no evil thing will ever happen: and forty days before the death of person who has this Oration about him or her, the Blessed

Virgin will appear to him or her. So said St. Gregorius.

To all those faithful who shall recite for 3 years, each day 2 Our Fathers, 2 Glory be's, and 2 Hail Marys, in honour of the drops of blood I lost, I will concede the following 5 graces;

1st   The plenary indulgence and remittance of your sins.

2nd You will be free from the pains of Purgatory.

3rd If you should die before completing the said 3 years, for you it will be the same as if you had completed them.

4th It will be upon your death the same as if you had shed all your blood for the Holy Faith.

5th I will descend from Heaven to take your soul and that of your relatives, until the fourth generation

Be it known that the number of armed soldiers were 150; those who trailed me while I was bound were 23. The executioners of justice were

83; the blows received on my head were 150; those on my stomach, 108; kicks on my shoulders, 80. I was led, bound with cords by the hair, 24 times; spits in the face were 180; I was beaten on the body 6666 times; beaten on the head, 110 times. I was roughly pushed, and at 12 o'clock was lifted up by the hair; pricked with thorns and pulled by the beard 23 times; received 20 wounds on the head; thorns of marine junks, 72; pricks of thorns in the head, ll0; mortal thorns in the forehead, 3. I was afterwards flogged and dressed as a mocked king; wounds in the body, 1000. The soldiers who led me to the Calvary were 608; those who watched me were 3, and those who mocked me were 1008; the drops of blood which I lost were 28,430.

Benedetta DA S.S, Pope Leo XIII, In Roma 5 Aprile 1890

PRAYER TO THE INFANT OF PRAGUE

O merciful Infant Jesus, I know of Your miraculous deeds for the sick. In view of the innumerable graces and the cures granted through the veneration of Your Holy Infancy, particularly in the statue of Prague, I exclaim with the greatest assurance: O most loving Infant Jesus, You can cure me if You will! Extend Your holy hand and by Your power take away all pain and infirmity!

INFANT OF PRAGUE

The more you honour Me, the more I will bless you! "Occupy yourself with My interests and I will occupy Myself with yours"

Our Lord to St. Teresa of Avila.

Devotion to the Infant Jesus is as old as Christianity itself. It ever tends to keep the great mystery of our Lord's birth vividly before us.

A special devotion to the Divine Child originated with the Carmelites in the city of Prague, Bohemia, in the beginning of the seventeenth century. Princess Polyxenia of Lobkowitz had received as a wedding gift from her mother - a statue of the Divine Child, previously brought from Spain. After the death of her husband, the princess devoted herself to works of charity and was particularly helpful to the Carmelites in Prague. When in 1628 the Carmelite Monastery had been reduced to poverty, owing to the ravages of war, the princess gave her precious statue to the Carmelites, saying:

"I GIVE YOU WHAT I PRIZE MOST HIGHLY IN THE WORLD; HONOUR AND RESPECT THE CHILD JESUS AND YOU SHALL NEVER BE IN WANT."

Her gift was placed in the Carmelite oratory. The words of the princess proved prophetic for as long as the Carmelites kept up their devotion to the Divine Infant of Prague everything prospered with them. The Carmelites were later forced to flee from the city and in the confusion of the war they were unable to take with them their miraculous statue. The invaders seized it and threw it into a pile of rubbish.

In 1635, peace came to Prague and the Carmelites returned. One of them, Father Cyril, who had previously received great spiritual help through his devotion to the Infant of Prague, sought the statue and found it amidst the rubbish. Overjoyed, he placed the statue again in the oratory. As Father Cyril was one day praying devotedly before the statue, he heard a voice saying. "HAVE MERCY ON ME AND I WILL HAVE MERCY ON YOU. RETURN MY HANDS TO ME AND I SHALL GIVE YOU PEACE, THE MORE YOU HONOUR ME, THE MORE I SHALL BLESS YOU". Startled by these words, Father Cyril examined the statue and upon drawing aside the mantle covering it, he found that both hands of the statue were broken off. The hands were restored to the statue through the generosity of a devotee of the Divine Child. Once more peace and prosperity returned to the Carmelites.

Devotion to the Divine Child had always been practiced by the Carmelites for through their Mother, Mary, this Divine Child had come to the world. St. Theresa of Jesus practiced particular devotion to the Divine Child. St. Therese, the Little Flower, was also a most fervent venerator.

PRAYERS AFTER MASS AND COMMUNION

Prayer Before a Crucifix

Look down upon me good and gentle Jesus, while before Thy face I humbly kneel and with burning soul pray and beseech Thee to fix deep in my heart lively sentiments of faith, hope and charity, true contrition for my sins and a firm purpose of amendment, while I contemplate with great love and tender pity Thy Five Wounds, pondering over them within me and calling to mind the words which David Thy prophet said of Thee my Jesus, "They have pierced My Hands and My Feet, they have numbered all My Bones."(Ps. 21,17-18)

Our Father, Hail Mary, Glory Be, for Holy Father's intentions.

Plenary indulgence when said after Communion: (S. Paen. Ap., 2 Feb. 1934)

ANIMA CHRISTI

Soul of Christ, sanctify me
Body of Christ, save me.
Blood of Christ, inebriate me.
Water from the side of Christ, wash me.
Passion of Christ, strengthen me.
O good Jesus, hear me
Within Thy wounds hide me.
Suffer me not to be separated from Thee
From the malignant enemy, defend me.
In the hour of my death, call me.
And bid me come to Thee.
That with Thy saints I may praise Thee.
Forever and ever Amen.

An indulgence of 300 days; an indulgence of 7 years, if
recited after Holy Communion (St. Ignatius Loyola).

Rosary of the Holy Wounds of Our Lord Jesus Christ or Chaplet of Mercy

May Be Said on the Rosary Beads

On the large beads: Eternal Father, I offer Thee
the WOUNDS of Our Lord Jesus Christ - To heal
the wounds of our souls.

(300 days indulgence each time).

On the small beads: My Jesus, pardon and mercy

Through the merits of Thy HOLY WOUNDS
(300 days indulgence each time).

Sacred Penitentiary, January 15, 1924

These two invocations were taught by Our Lord to Sr. M. Martha Chambon, deceased, in the Visitation of Chambery, France, March 21, 1907. The Sister received from Our Lord a double "Mission": constantly to invoke the HOLY WOUNDS herself and to revive this devotion in the world.

Promises of Our Lord to Sr. Mary Martha

"I will grant all that is asked of Me by the invocation of My HOLY WOUNDS. You must spread the devotion."

PRAYER TO DEFEAT THE WORK OF SATAN

O Divine Eternal Father, In union with your Divine Son and the Holy Spirit, and through the Immaculate Heart of Mary, I beg You to destroy the Power of your greatest enemy - the evil spirits.

Cast them into the deepest recesses of hell and chain them there forever! Take possession of your Kingdom which You have created and which is rightfully yours.

Heavenly Father, give us the reign of the Sacred Heart of Jesus and the Immaculate Heart of Mary.

I repeat this prayer out of pure love for You with every beat of my heart and with every breath I take. Amen.

Imprimatur, March 1973, Richard H. Ackerman, Bishop of Covington.

DEVOTIONS AND PRAYERS

TAKE TIME TO PRAY...
It is the greatest power on earth !

WHEN YOU PRAY...
"Say what you mean and mean what you say."

"Pray without ceasing"

THE JESUS PRAYER

"Lord Jesus Christ, have mercy on me"
(say 600 times a day)

"GOD GOVERNS THE WORLD
BUT PRAYER GOVERNS GOD"

In the name of the Father and of the Son and of the Holy Spirit. Amen.

Come Holy Ghost, fill the hearts of Thy faithful and enkindle in them the fire of Thy love.
V. Send forth Thy Spirit and They shall be created.
R. And Thou shalt renew the face of the earth.

Let us pray:
O God, who by the light of the Holy Spirit, didst instruct the hearts of the faithful grant that in the same Spirit we may be truly wise and ever rejoice in His consolation, through Christ Our Lord. Amen.

Indulgence of five years. Plenary indulgences, under the usual conditions, if the prayer has been recited daily for a month. Enclliridion Indulgenchiridiom, 287.

SAY DAILY UPON ARISING;
7 Glory Be's to the Holy Ghost

CHAPLET OF FAITH

On each decade of the rosary pray:

-on large bead: One Apostles Creed
-on 10 small beads: Jesus, Mary, I love you, save souls, save the consecrated
- at the end, 5 times: Hail Holy Queen

Blessed Virgin Mary to Saint Dominic, "One Day through the Rosary and Scapular I will save the World."
"Whosoever dies clothed in this (scapular) shall not suffer eternal fire."

This is Mary's Promise made July 16, 1251 to Saint Simon Stock.

The devils revealed to Francis of Yepes, the brother of St. John of the Cross, that three things especially tormented them. The first is the name of Jesus, the second the name of Mary, and the third the brown scapular of Our Lady of Mt. Carmel. "Take off that habit" they cried to him, which snatches so many souls from us. All those clothed in it die piously and escape us. Your SCAPULAR, then should take on deep meaning for you. It is a rich present brought down from Heaven by

OUR LADY HERSELF

"Wear it devoutly and perseveringly" she says to each soul, "it is my garment. To be clothed in it means you are continually thinking of me, and I in turn, am always thinking of you and helping you to secure eternal life."

Prayer of St. Simon Stock

Known as the FLOS CARMELI, the following prayer has for seven centuries been called a prayer to the Blessed Mother which has never been known to fail in obtaining her powerful help.

Prayer

O beautiful Flower of Carmel, most fruitful vine, Splendour of Heaven, Holy and singular, who brought forth the Son of God, still ever remaining a Pure Virgin, assist me in this necessity. O Star of the Sea, help and protect me! Show me that Thou are my Mother.

O Mary, conceived without sin,
Pray for us who have recourse to thee!

Mother and Ornament of Carmel, Pray for us!
Virgin, Flower of Carmel, Pray for us!
Patroness of all who wear the Scapular, Pray for us! Hope of all who die wearing the Scapular, Pray for us!

St. Joseph, Friend of the Sacred Heart, Pray for us! St. Joseph, Chaste Spouse of Mary, Pray for us! St. Joseph, Our Patron, Pray for us!

O sweet Heart of Mary, Be our Salvation!

The Fifteen Promises of Mary to Christians Who Recite the Rosary

1. Whoever shall faithfully serve me by the recitation of the rosary, shall receive signal graces.
2. I promise my special protection and the greatest graces to all those who shall recite the rosary.
3. The rosary shall be a powerful armour against hell, it will destroy vice, decrease sin, and defeat heresies.
4. It will cause virtue and good works to flourish; it will obtain for souls the abundant mercy of God; it will withdraw the hearts of men from the love of the world and its vanities and will lift them to the desire of eternal things. Oh, those souls would sanctify themselves by these means.

5. The soul which recommends itself to me by the recitation of the rosary, shall not perish.

6. Whoever shall recite the rosary devoutly, applying himself to the consideration of its sacred mysteries shall never be conquered by misfortune. God will not chastise him in His justice, he shall not perish by an unprovided death; if he be just, he shall remain in the grace of God, and become worthy of eternal life.

7. Whoever shall have a true devotion for the rosary shall not die without the sacraments of the Church.

8. Those who are faithful to recite the rosary shall have during their life and at their death the light of God and the plenitude of His graces; at the moment of death they shall participate in the merits of the saints in paradise.

9. I shall deliver from purgatory those who have been devoted to the rosary.

10. The faithful children of the rosary shall merit a high degree of glory in heaven.

11. You shall obtain all you ask of me by the recitation of the rosary.

12. All those who propagate the holy rosary shall be aided by me in their necessities.

13. I have obtained from my Divine Son that all the advocates of the rosary shall have for intercessors the entire celestial court during their life and at the hour of death.

14. All who recite the rosary are my sons and brothers of my only son Jesus Christ.
15. Devotion of my rosary is a great sign of predestination. *(Given to St. Dominic and Blessed Alan) Imprimatur +PATRICK J. HAYES, D.D. , Archbishop of New York*

WHY the daily rosary ?

Our Lady has 117 titles. She selected this title at Fatima: "I am the Lady of the Rosary"
St. Francis de Sales said the greatest method of praying IS - Pray the Rosary.
St. Thomas Aquinas preached 40 straight days in Rome, Italy on just the Hail Mary.
St John Vianney, patron of priests, was seldom seen without a rosary in his hand.
"The rosary is the scourge of the devil." - Pope Adrian VI.
"The Rosary is a treasure of graces."-Pope Paul V.
Padre Pio the stigmatic priest said:
"The Rosary is **THE WEAPON**"
Pope Leo XIII wrote 9 encyclicals on the rosary.
Pope John XXIII spoke 38 times about our Lady and the Rosary. He prayed 15 decades daily.
St. Louis Marie Grignion de Montfort wrote:
"The Rosary is the most powerful weapon to touch the Heart of Jesus, Our Redeemer, who so loves His Mother"

If you wish to obtain a favour, pray the "54 days ROSARY NOVENA":

Pray 3 nine day rosary novenas - 27 days of petition;

Pray 3 nine day rosary novenas - 27 days of thanksgiving.

Will you give 1% of 1440 minutes each day to God? If so, pray the daily rosary in 15 minutes - 1% of 24 hours.

Later on, give 3% and pray entire 15 decade rosary. Joyful, Sorrowful and Glorious Mysteries.

"WHY should I Go To Mass Every Day?"
"The Mass is the most perfect form of prayer!"
(Pope Paul VI)

For each Mass we hear with devotion, Our Lord sends a saint to comfort us at death. (Revelation of Christ to St. Gertrude the Great).

Padre Pio, the stigmatic priest, said, the world could exist more easily without the sun than without the Mass.

The Cure d'Ars, St. Jean Vianney said, "if we knew the value of the Mass we would die of joy."

A great doctor of the Church, St. Anselm, declares that a single Mass offered for oneself during life may be worth more than a thousand celebrated for the same intention after death. St. Leonard of Port Maurice supports this statement by saying that one Mass before death may be more profitable than many after it.

The Holy Mass would be of greater profit if people had it offered in their lifetime, rather than having it celebrated for the relief of their souls after death. (Pope Benedict XV)

Once, St. Theresa was overwhelmed with God's Goodness and asked Our Lord, "How can I thank you?" Our Lord replied, "ATTEND ONE MASS"

The Blessed Virgin Mary once told Her faithful servant Alain: "My Son so loves those who assist at the Holy Sacrifice of the Mass that, if it were necessary, He would die for them as many times as they've heard Masses."

Page 107, last paragraph of "Explication Du Saint Sacrifice De La Messe" parle R.P. Martin de Cochem Friere Mineur Capucin.)

"Jesus, Mary, I love You, save Souls"

A SHORT WAY OF THE CROSS

**As used by
The Franciscan Fathers on their Missions**

First Station
Jesus Condemned to Death
O Jesus, so meek and uncomplaining, teach me
resignation in trials.

Second Station
Jesus Carries His Cross
My Jesus, this Cross should be mine, not Thine;
my sins crucified Thee.

Third Station
Our Lord Falls the First Time
O Jesus, by this first fall, never let me fall into
mortal sin.

Fourth Station
Jesus Meets His Mother
O Jesus, may no human tie, however dear, keep
me from following the road of the Cross.

Fifth Station
Simon the Cyrenean Helps Jesus carry His Cross
Simon unwillingly assisted Thee;
may I with patience suffer all for Thee.

Sixth Station
Veronica Wipes the Face of Jesus
O Jesus, Thou didst imprint Thy sacred features upon Veronica's veil, stamp them also indelibly upon my heart.

Seventh Station
The Second Fall of Jesus
By Thy second fall, preserve me, dear Lord, from relapse into sin.

Eighth Station
Jesus Consoles the Woman of Jerusalem
My greatest consolation would be to hear Thee say: "Many sins are forgiven thee, because thou hast loved much".

Ninth Station
Third Fall of Jesus
O Jesus, when weary upon life's long journey, be Thou my strength and my perseverance.

Tenth Station
Jesus Stripped of His Garments
My soul has been robbed of its robe of innocence; clothe me, dear Jesus, with the garb of penance and contrition.

Eleventh Station
Jesus nailed to the Cross
Thou didst forgive Thy enemies; my God, teach me to forgive injuries and FORGET them.

Twelfth Station
Jesus Dies on the Cross
Thou art dying, my Jesus, but Thy Sacred Heart throbs with love for Thy sinful children.

Thirteenth Station
Jesus Taken Down from the Cross
Receive me into thy arms, O Sorrowful Mother; and obtain for me perfect contrition for my sins.

Fourteenth Station
Jesus Laid in the Sepulchre
When I receive Thee into my heart in Holy Communion, O Jesus, make it a fit abiding place for Thy adorable Body. Amen.

"Jesus, Mary, I love You, Save Souls"

The 4 keys to Heaven

MASS
ROSARY
SCAPULAR
WAY OF THE CROSS

"Jesus, Mary, I love you, Save Souls"

At the age of 18, a young Spaniard entered the Novitiate of the Brothers of the Christian Schools at Bugedo. He took the Vow of Regularity, Perfection and Pure Love. In October, 1926, he offered himself to Jesus through Mary. Soon after this heroic donation, he fell ill, and was obliged to rest. He died saintly in March 1927. He was, according to the Master of Novices, a Privileged Soul, who received Messages from Heaven. Confessors and Theologians recognised these Supernatural facts. His Director asked him to write the Promises made by OUR LORD to those who have devotion to THE WAY OF THE CROSS; They are:

1. I'll grant everything that's asked of Me with Faith, when making The Way of The Cross.
2. I promise Eternal Life to those who pray from time to time, The Way of The Cross.
3. I'll follow them everywhere in life and I'll help them, especially at the hour of death.
4. Even if they have more sins than blades of grass in the fields and grains of sand in the sea, all of them will be erased by The Way of The Cross. (Note: This promise doesn't eliminate the obligation to confess all mortal sins, before we can receive Holy Communion.)
5. Those who pray The Way of The Cross often, will have a special glory in Heaven.

6. I'll deliver them from Purgatory, indeed if they go there at all, the first Tuesday or Friday after their death.

7. I'll bless them at each Way of The Cross, and My blessing will follow them everywhere on earth and, after their death, in Heaven for all Eternity.

8. At the hour of death I won't permit the devil to tempt them; I'll lift all power from him in order that they'll repose tranquilly in My Arms.

9. If they pray it with true love, I'll make of each one of them a living Ciborium in which it will please Me to pour My Grace.

10. I'll fix My Eyes on those who pray The Way of The Cross often; My hands will always be open to protect them.

11. As I am nailed to the Cross, so also will I always be with those who honour Me in making The Way of The Cross frequently.

12. They'll never be able to separate themselves from Me, for I'll give them the grace never again to commit a Mortal sin.

13. At the hour of death I'll console them with My Presence and we'll go together to Heaven. Death will be sweet to all those who have honoured Me during their lives by praying The Way of The Cross.

14. My Soul will be a protective shield for them, and will always help them, whenever they have recourse.

"Jesus, Mary, I love You, Save Souls"

St. Alphonsus Liguori wrote, *If you pray you are sure of saving your soul. If you do not pray you are just as sure to lose your soul.*

Prayer to the Shoulder Wound of Christ

O loving Jesus, meek Lamb of God, I miserable sinner, salute and worship the most Sacred Wound of Your Shoulder on which You did bear Your heavy Cross, which so tore Your flesh and laid bare Your Bones as to inflict on You anguish greater than any other wound of Your Most Blessed Body. I adore You, O Jesus most sorrowful: I praise and glorify You, and give You thanks for this most sacred and painful Wound, beseeching You by that exceeding pain, and by the crushing burden of Your heavy Cross to be merciful to me, a sinner, to forgive me all my mortal and venial sins, and lead me on towards Heaven along the Way of Your Cross. Amen.

+Imprimatur:

+Thomas D. Bevan
Bishop of
Springfield

It is related in the annals of Clairvaux that St. Bernard asked our Lord which was His greatest unrecorded suffering and Our Lord answered: "I had on My Shoulder, while I bore My Cross on the Way of Sorrows, a grievous Wound, which was more painful than the others, and which is not recorded by men.

Honour this wound with your devotion, and I will grant you whatsoever you'd ask through its virtue and merit. And in regard to all those who shall venerate this Wound, I will remit to them all their venial sins, and will no longer remember their mortal sins".

"Jesus, Mary, I love You, Save Souls".

INVOCATIONS IN HONOUR OF THE HOLY WOUNDS OF OUR LORD JESUS CHRIST

Eternal Father I offer You the Wounds of Our Lord Jesus Christ to heal the wounds of our souls. My Jesus, pardon and mercy through the merits of Your Sacred Wounds.

Sister Mary Martha Chambon, a humble lay Sister of the Visitation Order of Chambery, France, who died in the odour of sanctity, March 21st, 1907, received these two invocations from Our Lord Himself, as she affirmed, and with them a double MISSION to adore and invoke the Sacred Wounds unceasingly and to revive this devotion in the hearts of creatures.

Our Lord said:

"The soul who during life has honoured and studied the Wounds of Our Lord Jesus Christ, and has offered them to the Eternal Father for the souls in Purgatory, will be accompanied at the moment of death by the Holy Virgin and the angels; and Our Lord on the Cross all brilliant in glory will receive them and crown them".

"Jesus, Mary, I Love You, Save Souls"

PRAY FOR SOULS IN PURGATORY

There are more souls released from purgatory during consecration of the Mass than at any time. Christmas is the day of the year when most souls are delivered: then feast days of Our Lord, Our Lady and great saints. Souls receive much grace from prayers offered for them on their birthdays, day of baptism, anniversary of death.

The more we work for Poor Souls on earth the more others will pray for us, and more merciful will Christ be with us when we're in purgatory.

Our Lady asked that we pray very much for the poor souls; that we pray:

5 **I believe in God...**

1 **Hail Holy Queen...**

1 **Our Father...**

1 **Hail Mary...**

1 **Glory be to the Father...**

1 **Requiem** (Eternal rest grant unto them, O Lord

and let perpetual light shine upon them and may they rest in peace. Amen!)

Our Lady said that if we pray the prayers "we'll deliver so many souls, so many souls!"

"The Holy wounds are the treasure of treasures for the souls in Purgatory".

"Jesus, Mary, I love You, Save Souls."

BIBLE - 2 Machabees, Chaper 12, Verse 46:

"it is therefore a holy and wholesome thought to pray for the dead, that they may be loosed from sins".

An Indulgence applicable only to the souls, in purgatory is granted when the faithful devoutly visit a cemetary and pray for the dead.

THE SPIRITUAL COMMUNION

By a rescript of November 24, 1922 the Sacred Congregation of Indulgences approved the following formula for a spiritual Communion.

"O Jesus I turn towards the holy tabernacle where You live hidden for love of me. I love you, O my God. I cannot receive You in Holy Communion. Come nevertheless and visit me with Your Grace. Come spiritually into my heart. Purify it. Sanctify it. Render it like unto Your own. Amen."

Lord, I am not worthy that You should enter under my roof, but only say the word and my soul shall be healed.

An indulgence of 500 days, if thrice repeated. (129 The Raccolta 1944).

It was the Cure of Ars who said, "A Spiritual Communion acts on the soul as blowing does on a cinder-covered fire which was about to go out. Whenever you feel your love of God growing cold, quickly make a Spiritual Communion".

MESSAGE OF WORLDWIDE IMPORTANCE

Devotion to the Sorrowful and Immaculate Heart of Mary

This Message was confided by Our Lord to Berthe Petit, a humble Franciscan Tertiary, Born on January 23, 1870, at Enghien, Belgium:

"Teach souls to love the Heart of My Mother pierced by the very sorrows which pierced Mine." (December 25, 1909)

At the Holy Hour (March 25, 1912) the Blessed Virgin spoke thus: "I have called myself the Immaculate Conception. To you I call myself Mother of the Sorrowful Heart. This title willed by my Son is dear to me above all others. According as it is spread everywhere, there will be granted graces of mercy, spiritual renewal and salvation."

❖   ❖   ❖   ❖

PRAYER
(Composed by Berthe Petit)

Sorrowful and Immaculate Heart of Mary, dwelling pure and holy, cover my soul with your maternal protection so that being ever faithful to the voice of Jesus, it responds to His love and obeys His Divine Will.

I wish, O, My Mother, to keep unceasingly before me your co-redemption in order to live intimately with your Heart that is totally united to the Heart of your Divine Son.

Fasten me to this Heart by your own virtues and sorrows. Protect me always.

The Prayer or Blessing Against Storms
is of great importance

Jesus Christ a King of Glory has come in Peace †
God became man † and the Word was made flesh. †
Christ was born of a Virgin. † Christ suffered. †
Christ was crucified. † Christ died. † Christ rose
from the dead. † Christ ascended into Heaven. †
Christ conquers. † Christ reigns. † Christ orders. †
May Christ protect us from all storms and lightning.
† Christ went through their midst in Peace † and the
word was made flesh. † Christ is with us with Mary.
† Flee you enemy spirits because the Lion of the
Generation of Juda, the Root David, has won. †
Holy God. † Holy Powerful God. † Holy Immortal
God. † Have mercy on us. Amen!

Above, in Millet's famous painting, a peasant boy and girl in France recite the Angelus at dark. "The angel of the Lord declared unto Mary..."

It is one of the most famous paintings in the world.

6-12-6

THE ANGELUS

V. The Angel of the Lord declared unto Mary

R. And she conceived of the Holy Ghost. ("Hail Mary" Prayer) V. Behold the handmaid of the Lord.

R. Be it done unto me according to thy word. ("Hail Mary" Prayer)

V. And the Word was made flesh.

R. And dwelt among us ("Hail Mary")

V. Pray for us, O holy Mother of God.

R. That we may be made worthy of the promises of Christ.

Let us pray: Pour forth, we beseech Thee, O Lord, Thy grace into our hearts, that we to whom the Incarnation of Christ, Thy Son, was made known by the message of an angel, may by His passion and cross be brought to the glory of His resurrection, through the same Christ Our Lord. Amen.

"Jesus, Mary, I love You, Save Souls."

PRAYER TO ST. MICHAEL

St. Michael the Archangel, defend us in the day of battle. Be our safeguard against the wickedness and snares of the Devil. May God rebuke Him, we humbly pray, and do Thou, O Prince of the Heavenly Host, by the power of God, cast into Hell, Satan and all other evil spirits, who prowl through the world, seeking the ruin of souls. Amen.

The Raccolta 447. An indulgence of 3 years.

(This powerful prayer of exorcism was composed by Pope Leo XIII; in a vision, he had been shown the fearful battle to be waged between Satan and St. Michael, over the Church of the future. Now, as never before, the Church needs the intercession of St. Michael! Please say this prayer every day.)

MARY, QUEEN OF THE HOLY ANGELS PRAY FOR US!

"Jesus, Mary, I love You, Save Souls"

Sincere Act of Contrition

Saint Michael appearing one day to Antonia d'Astonac, a most devout Servant of God, told her that he wished to be honoured by nine salutations corresponding to the nine Choirs of Angels, which should consist of one Our Father and three Hail Marys in honour of each of the angelic choirs.

Promises of St. Michael

Whosoever would practice this devotion in his honour would have, when approaching the Holy Table, an escort of nine angels chosen from each one of the nine choirs. In addition, for the daily recital of these nine salutations he promised his continual assistance and that of all the holy angels during life, and after death deliverance from purgatory for themselves and their relations.

Method of Reciting the Chaplet

The chaplet is begun by saying the following invocation on the medal: *O God, come to my assistance. O Lord, make haste to help me. Glory be to the Father, etc.*

Following the arrow on the diagram 1-9, say one Our Father and three Hail Marys after each of the following nine salutations in honour of the nine choirs of angels.

By the intercession of St. Michael and the celestial Choir of Seraphim, may the Lord make us worthy to burn with the fire of perfect charity. Amen.

2.

By the intercession of St. Michael and the celestial Choir of Cherubim, may the Lord vouchsafe to grant us grace to leave the ways of wickedness to run in the paths of Christian perfection. Amen.

3.

By the intercession of St. Michael and the celestial Choir of Thrones, may the Lord infuse into our hearts a true and sincere spirit of humility. Amen.

4.

By the intercession of St. Michael and the celestial Choir of Dominions, may the Lord give us grace to govern our senses and subdue our unruly passions. Amen.

5.

By the intercession of St. Michael and the celestial Choir of Powers, may the Lord vouchsafe to protect our souls against the snare and temptations of the devil. Amen.

6.

By the intercession of St. Michael and the celestial Choir of Virtues may the Lord preserve us from evil and suffer us not to fall into temptation. Amen.

7.

By the intercession of St. Michael and the celestial Choir of Principalities, may God fill our souls with a true spirit of obedience. Amen.

8.

By the intercession of St. Michael and the celestial Choir of Archangels, may the Lord give us perseverance in faith and in all good works, in order that we gain the glory of Paradise. Amen.

9.

By the intercession of St. Michael and the celestial Choir of Angels, may the Lord grant us to be protected by them in this mortal life and conducted hereafter to eternal glory. Amen.

Following the arrow on the diagram, *(10-13 on the beads closer to medal)*, say one Our Father in honour of each of the following leading angels:

10. St. Michael: 11 St. Gabriel: 12. St. Raphael. 13. Our Guardian Angel

The chaplet is concluded with the following prayers:

O Glorious Prince St. Michael, chief and commander of the heavenly hosts, guardian of souls, vanquisher of rebel spirits, servant in the house of the Divine King, and our admirable conductor, thou who dost shine with excellence and superhuman virtue, vouchsafe to deliver us from all evil, who turn to thee with confidence, and enable us by thy gracious protection to serve God more and more faithfully every day.

V. Pray for us, O glorious St. Michael, Prince of the Church of Jesus Christ.

R. That we may be made worthy of His Promises.

PRAYER

Almighty and Everlasting God, who by a prodigy of goodness and a merciful desire of the salvation of all people, hast appointed the most glorious Archangel St. Michael, Prince of Your Church, make us worthy, we beseech You to be delivered from all our enemies that none of them may harass us at the hour of death, but that we may be conducted by him into the august presence of Your Divine Majesty. This we beg through the merits of Jesus Christ our Lord. Amen. (With Ecclesiastical Approval)

CHAPLET BEADS OF ST. MICHAEL
may be obtained from
Divine Mercy Publications
Maryville, Skerries, Co Dublin.
Tel: 01- 8491458 Fax: 01-8492466

SALVE REGINA
Hail, Holy Queen

Hail, Holy Queen, Mother of Mercy, Hail our life, our sweetness and our hope! To thee do we cry, poor banished children of Eve: to thee do we send up our sighs, mourning and weeping in this valley of tears. Turn then, most gracious advocate, thine eyes of mercy towards us and after this our exile, show unto us the blessed fruit of thy womb, Jesus. O clement, O loving, O sweet Virgin Mary. Pray for us O Holy Mother of God, that we may be made worthy of the promises of Christ. Amen.

It may be prayed standing - or arms extended - or sung.

"An indulgence of 5 years."

DAILY PRAYER TO GUARDIAN ANGEL

Angel of God
My guardian dear
To Whom God's Love
Commits me here

Ever this day
Be at my side
To light and guard
To rule and guide.
Amen.

"Say daily upon arising, 7 Glory Be's to your guardian angel"

"The Little Flower"

"I wish to spend my heaven
in doing good upon earth"

To Saint Therese of the Child Jesus and the Holy Face asking for necessary favours.

ORIGIN OF THE NOVENA

Father Putigan, a Jesuit, began the Novena to Saint Therese of the Child Jesus on December 3, 1925, asking the glorious Saint for one great favour. For nine days he recited the "Glory be to the Father" twenty-four times thanking the Holy Trinity for the favours and Graces showered on Saint Therese during the twenty-four years of her life on earth. The priest asked Saint Therese that as a sign that his novena was heard, he would receive from someone a freshly plucked rose. On the third day of the novena, an unknown person sought out Father Putigan and presented him with a beautiful rose.

Father Putigan began the second novena on December 24 of the same year, and as a sign, asked for a white rose. On the fourth day of this novena one of the Sister - Nurses brought him a white rose saying:

"Saint Therese sent you this."
Amazed, the priest asked:
"Where did you get this?"
"I was in the chapel", said the Sister

"and as I was leaving I passed the altar above which hangs the beautiful picture of Saint Therese. This rose fell at my feet. I wanted to put it back into the bouquet, but a thought came to me that I should bring it to you".

Father Putigan received the favours he had petitioned of the Little Flower of Jesus, and promised to spread the novena to increase devotion to, and bring her more honour.

In this fashion, from the ninth to the seventeenth of each month, those who want to participate in the Twenty-four "Glory be to the Father's" novena, should add to those of their own, the intentions of all who are at the time making the novena, thus forming one great prayer in common.

THE NOVENA

The Twenty-four "Glory be to the Father's" novena can be said at any time. However, the ninth to the seventeenth of the month is particularly recommended, for on those days the petitioner joins in prayer with all those making the novena.

Between the Glory Be's, say "Saint Therese of the Child Jesus, pray for us"

ST. THERESE,
THE LITTLE FLOWER,
PLEASE PICK ME A ROSE
FROM THE HEAVENLY GARDEN
AND SEND IT TO ME
WITH A MESSAGE OF LOVE
ASK GOD TO GRANT ME THE
FAVOUR I THEE IMPLORE AND
TELL HIM I WILL LOVE
HIM EACH DAY MORE AND MORE

(The above prayer, plus 5 Our Fathers, 5 Hail Mary's, 5 Glory Be's, must be said on 5 successive days, before eleven a.m. On the 5th day, the 5th set of prayers having been completed, offer one more set - 5 Our Father's, 5 Hail Mary's, 5 Glory Be's)

TRY IT - IT WORKS

FACE OF JESUS
FROM HOLY SHROUD OF TURIN

PRAYER

(Composed by St. Therese of Lisieux)

Jesus, Who in Thy bitter Passion didst become "the reproach of men and the Man of Sorrows", I venerate Thy Holy Face on which shone the beauty and gentleness of Divinity. In those disfigured features I recognise Thine infinite love, and I long to love Thee and to make Thee loved...May I behold Thy Glorious Face in Heaven!

(St. Therese's name in Religion was Therese of the Child Jesus and the Holy Face) +Imprimatur: JOANNES HENRICUS Ep. Portus Magni Die 3 Oct. 1958.

"Jesus, Mary, I love You, Save Souls"

The Golden Arrow

May the most holy, most sacred, most adorable, most mysterious and unutterable Name of God be always praised, blessed, loved, adored and glorified in Heaven on earth and under the earth, by all the creatures of God, and by the Sacred Heart of our Lord Jesus Christ in the most Holy Sacrament of the altar.

This prayer was revealed by Our Lord to a Carmelite Nun of Tours in 1843 as a reparation for blasphemy. "This Golden Arrow will wound My Heart delightfully", He said, "and heal the wounds inflicted by blasphemy", +Imprimatur T.J.Toolen, Archbishop of Mobile-Birm

THE CHAPLET OF THE DIVINE MERCY

Jesus I Trust in You

The Lord said to Saint Faustina (1905-1938): You will recite this chaplet on the beads of the rosary in the following manner:

First of all you will say one **OUR FATHER**, one **HAIL MARY**, and one **APOSTLES CREED.**

Then, on the **OUR FATHER BEADS** say these words:

"Eternal Father, I offer You the Body and Blood, Soul and Divinity of Your Dearly Beloved Son our Lord Jesus Christ, in atonement for our sins and those of the whole world."

On the **HAIL MARY BEADS** say the following words:
For the sake of His sorrowful Passion have mercy on us and on the whole world.

At the end of five decades say

**Holy God,
Holy Mighty One,
Holy Immortal One,
have mercy on us and
on the whole world.**

Here is your formula of

by St. Louis De Montfort

Eternal and Incarnate Wisdom! O sweetest and most adorable Jesus! True God and true man, only Son of the Eternal Father, and of Mary, always Virgin! I adore Thee profoundly in the bosom and splendors of Thy Father during eternity: and I adore Thee also in the virginal bosom of Mary, Thy most worthy Mother, in the time of Thine Incarnation.

I give Thee thanks for that Thou hast annihilated Thyself, taking the form of a slave in order to rescue me from the cruel slavery of the devil. I praise and glorify Thee for that Thou hast been pleased to submit Thyself to Mary, Thy holy Mother, in all things, in order to make me Thy faithful slave through her. But Alas! Ungrateful and faithless as I have been, I have not kept the promises which I made so solemnly to Thee in my Baptism. I have not fulfiled my obligations: I do not deserve to be called Thy child, nor yet Thy slave; and as there is nothing in me which does not merit Thine anger and Thy repulse, I dare not come by myself before Thy most holy and august majesty. It is on this account that I have recourse to the intercession of Thy most holy Mother, whom Thou hast given me for a mediatrix with Thee. It is through her that I hope to obtain of Thee contrition, the pardon of my sins and the acquisition and preservation of wisdom.

Hail, then, O Immaculate Mary, living tabernacle of the Divinity, where the Eternal Wisdom willed to be hidden and to be adored by angels and by men! Hail, O Queen of Heaven and Earth, to whose empire everything is subject which is under God. Hail, O sure refuge of sinners, whose mercy fails no one. Hear the desires which I have of the Divine Wisdom: and for that end receive the vows and offerings which in my lowliness I present to You. I (your name) a faithless sinner, renew and ratify today in Your hands the vows of my Baptism; I renounce forever Satan, his pomps and works; and I give myself entirely to Jesus Christ, the Incarnate Wisdom, to carry my cross after him all the days of my life, and to be more faithful to Him than I have ever been before.

In the presence of all the heavenly court I choose You this day for my Mother and mistress. I deliver and consecrate to You, as Your slave, my body and soul, my goods, both interior and exterior, and even the value of all my good actions, past, present and future; leaving to You the entire full right of disposing of me, and all that belongs to me, without exception, according to Your good pleasure, for the greater glory of God in time and in eternity.

Receive, O benign Virgin, this little offering of my slavery, in honour of, and in union with that subjection which the Eternal Wisdom deigned to have to Your maternity, in homage to the power which both of you have over this poor sinner, and in thanksgiving for the privileges with which the Holy Trinity has favoured You. I declare that I wish henceforth, as Your true slave, to seek Your honour and to obey You in all things.

O admirable Mother, present me to Your dear Son as His eternal slave, so that as he has redeemed me by You, by You He may receive me! O Mother of mercy, grant me the grace to obtain the true Wisdom of God; and for that end receive among those whom You love and teach, whom You lead, nourish and protect as Your children and Your slaves.

O faithful Virgin, make me in all things so perfect a disciple, imitator and slave of the Incarnate Wisdom, Jesus Christ thy Son, that I may attain, by thine intercession and by thine example, to the fullness of His age on earth and His glory in Heaven. Amen.

(a plenary indulgence, under the usual conditions, on the feast of the Immaculate Conception and April 28 - Preces et Pia Opera, 75.)

"Jesus, Mary, I love You, Save Souls."

CATENA LEGIONIS

Antiphon - Who is she that cometh forth as the morning rising, fair as the moon, bright as the Sun, terrible as an army set in battle array ?

My soul doth magnify the Lord.

And my spirit hath rejoiced in God my Saviour.

Because He hath regarded the humility of His handmaid: for behold from henceforth all generation shall call me blessed.

For He that is mighty hath done great things to me, and holy is His name.

And His mercy is from generation unto generations to them that fear Him.

He hath showed might in His arm: He hath scattered the proud in the conceit of their heart.

He hath put down the mighty from their seat: and hath exalted the humble.

He hath filled the hungry with good things: and the rich He Has sent empty away.

He hath received Israel His servant: being mindful of His mercy.

As he spoke to our fathers: to Abraham and to his seed forever.

Glory be to the Father, and to the Son, and to the Holy Ghost .

As it was in the beginning, is now, and ever shall be, world without end. Amen.

Antiphon - Who is she that cometh forth as the morning rising, fair as the moon, bright as the sun, terrible as an army set in battle array?

V. O Mary conceived without sin.
R. Pray for us who have recourse to Thee.

Let us pray

O Lord Jesus Christ our Mediator with the Father, who hast been pleased to appoint the Most Blessed Virgin, Thy Mother, to be our Mother also, and our Mediatrix with Thee, mercifully grant that whosoever comes to Thee seeking Thy favours may rejoice to receive all of them through her.
Amen.

"Jesus, Mary, I love You, Save Souls."

A PRAYER FOR PRIESTS

Keep them, I pray thee, dearest Lord,
keep them for they are Thine -
Thy priests whose lives burn out before
Thy consecrated shrine.
Keep them, for they are in the world,
Though from the world apart
When earthly pleasures tempt, allure.
Shelter them in Thy heart.
Keep them, and comfort them in hours
Of loneliness and pain,
When all their life of sacrifice
For souls seems but in vain.
Keep them, and O remember, Lord,
They have no one but Thee,
Yet they have only human hearts,
With human frailty.
Keep them as spotless as the Host,
That daily they caress
Their every thought and word and deed
Deign, dearest Lord, to bless.

Imprimatur: +D. Card. Dougherty,
Arch. of Philadelphia

Our Father, Hail Mary,
Queen of the Clergy, pray for them.

THE PRIESTHOOD IS A MASTERPIECE OF
CHRIST'S DIVINE LOVE,
WISDOM AND POWER

NEVER ATTACK A PRIEST
"JESUS, MARY, I LOVE YOU, SAVE SOULS"

CRITICISM OF PRIESTS
Our Lord's revelations to Mutter Vogel

One should NEVER attack a priest, even when he's in error, rather one should pray and do penance that I'll grant him My grace again. He alone fully represents Me, even when he doesn't live after My example!" *(page 29, Mutter Vogel's Worldwide Love, St. Grignion Publishing House, Altoting, South Germany (29.6.1929).*

When a Priest falls we should extend him a helping hand **THROUGH PRAYER AND NOT THROUGH ATTACKS** I myself will be his judge, **NO ONE BUT I**! "Whoever voices judgement over a priest has voiced it over me: child, never let a Priest be attacked, take up his defence." (Feast of Christ and King 1937) "Child, Never judge your confessor, rather pray much for him and offer every Thursday, through the hands of My blessed Mother, Holy Communion (for Him) (18.6.1939) "Never again accept an out-of the-way word about a Priest, and speak no unkind word (about them) EVEN IF IT WERE TRUE! Every Priest is My Vicar and My heart will be sickened and insulted because of it! If you hear a judgement (against a Priest) pray a Hail Mary" (28.6.1939)

If you see a Priest who celebrates the Holy Mass unworthily then say nothing about him, rather tell it to Me alone! I stand beside Him on the altar!" O pray much for my priests, that they'll love purity above all, that they'll celebrate the Holy sacrifice of the Mass with pure hands and heart. Certainly the Holy Sacrifice is one and the same even when it's celebrated by an unworthy priest, but the graces called down upon the people is not the same!"(28. 2. 1938)

Mary, Queen of the Clergy, pray for them.

LITANY OF HUMILITY
(for private devotion only)

Which His Eminence Cardinal Merry del Val was accustomed to recite daily after the celebration of Holy Mass.

O Jesus! meek and humble of heart, hear me.
From the desire of being esteemed,
From the desire of being loved,
From the desire of being extolled,
From the desire of being honoured,
From the desire of being praised,
From the desire of being preferred,
From the desire of being consulted,
From the desire of being approved,
Deliver me, Jesus.
From the fear of being humiliated,
From the fear of being despised,
From the fear of suffering rebukes,
From the fear of being calumniated
From the fear of being forgotten,
From the fear of being ridiculed,

From the fear of being wronged,
From the fear of being suspected,
Deliver me, Jesus
That others may be loved more than I
That others may be esteemed more than I,
That in the opinion of the world, others may increase, and I may decrease,
That others may be chosen and I set aside,
That others may be praised and I unnoticed,
That others may be preferred to me in everything,
That others became holier than I, provided that I may become as holy as I should,

Jesus, grant me the grace to desire it.

Imprimatur: +James A . McNulty - Bishop of Paterson, N.J.

PRAYER TO THE SACRED HEAD OF OUR BLESSED LORD

As the Seat of Divine Wisdom.
WISDOM of the Sacred Head guide me in all my ways. O Love of the Sacred Heart, consume me with Thy fire. Three Glorias, In honour of the Divine Will, Memory and Understanding. O Seat of Divine Wisdom, and guiding Power, which governs all the motions and love of the Sacred Heart, may all minds know Thee all hearts love Thee and all tongues praise Thee, now and for evermore.

Imprimatur, Jacobus Canonicus Carr, Pro Epo Liverpolitano

Lord, have Mercy on Us. Christ, have Mercy on Us. Lord Have Mercy on Us.

Jesus, Graciously Hear Us.

God the Father of Heaven, have Mercy on Us.

God the Son Redeemer of the World, Have Mercy on Us.

God the Holy Spirit have Mercy on Us.

Sacred Head of Jesus Formed by the Holy Spirit in the Womb of the Virgin Mary.

(after each invocation say "GUIDE US IN ALL OUR WAYS")

Sacred Head of Jesus Substantially United to the Word of God,

Sacred Head of Jesus Temple of Divine Wisdom,

Sacred Head of Jesus, Centre of Eternal Light,

Sacred Head of Jesus Tabernacle of Divine Knowledge,

Sacred Head of Jesus Safeguard Against Error,

Sacred Head of Jesus Sunshine of Heaven and Earth,

Sacred Head of Jesus Treasure of Science and Pledge of Faith,

Sacred Head of Jesus Radiant With Beauty and Justice and Love,

Sacred Head of Jesus Full of Grace and Truth,

Sacred Head of Jesus Living Witness of Humility,

Sacred Head of Jesus Reflecting the Infinite Majesty of God,

Sacred Head of Jesus Centre of the Universe,

Sacred Head of Jesus Object of the Father's Joyous Satisfaction,

Sacred Head of Jesus Upon Which the Holy Ghost Rested,

Sacred Head of Jesus Around Which the Glory of Mt. Tabor Shone,

Sacred Head of Jesus Who Had No Place on Earth on Which to Rest,

Sacred Head of Jesus Whom the Fragrant Anointing of Magdalen Consoled,

Sacred Head of Jesus Bathed with the Sweat of Blood in Gethsemani,

Sacred Head of Jesus who Wept for our Sins,

Sacred Head of Jesus Crowned With Thorns,

Sacred Head of Jesus Outraged by the Indignities of the Passion,

Sacred Head of Jesus Consoled by the Loving Gesture of Veronica,

Sacred Head of Jesus Bowed to the Earth Which was Redeemed at the Moment of Death on Calvary, Guide Us in All Our Ways,

Sacred Head of Jesus Light of Every Being Born on Earth,

Sacred Head of Jesus Our Guide and Our Hope,

Sacred Head of Jesus Who Knows All our needs,

Sacred Head of Jesus Who Gives Us all Graces,

Sacred Head of Jesus That Governs All the Motions of the Sacred Heart,

Sacred Head of Jesus Whom we Wish to Adore And Make Known Throughout the World,

Sacred Head of Jesus Who Knows All the Secrets of Our Hearts,

Sacred Head of Jesus Who Enraptures Angels and the Saints,

Sacred Head of Jesus Whom One Day We Hope To Behold Unveiled for Ever,

Jesus, We Adore Your Sacred Head: We Surrender Utterly to All the Decrees of Your Infinite Wisdom.

EFFICACIOUS NOVENA TO THE SACRED HEART OF JESUS

I. Oh my Jesus, You said "Verily I say to You, ask and you shall receive, seek and you shall find, knock and it shall be opened to you", behold I knock, I seek and I ask for the grace of ...

Our Father, Hail Mary, Glory be to the Father, Sacred Heart of Jesus I put all my trust in Thee.

II. O my Jesus, You said, "Verily I say to You, whatsoever you shall ask the Father in My name, He will give it to you", behold in your name I ask the Father for the grace of...

Our Father, Hail Mary, Glory be to the Father. Sacred Heart of Jesus, I put all my trust in Thee.

III. O my Jesus, You said, "Verily I say to You, heaven and earth shall pass away but My words shall not pass away", behold I encouraged by your infallible words, now ask for the grace of.....

Our Father, Hail Mary, Glory be to the Father. Sacred Heart of Jesus, I put all my trust in Thee.

O Sacred Heart of Jesus, to whom one thing alone is impossible, namely, not to have compassion on the afflicted, have pity on us miserable sinners and grant us the grace which we ask of Thee through the Sorrowful and Immaculate Heart of Mary, Your tender Mother and ours.

Say the Salve Regina and add, **St. Joseph, foster father of Jesus, pray for us.**

P.S. - This novena prayer was recited every day by Padro Pio for all those who recommended themselves to his prayers.